T0017783

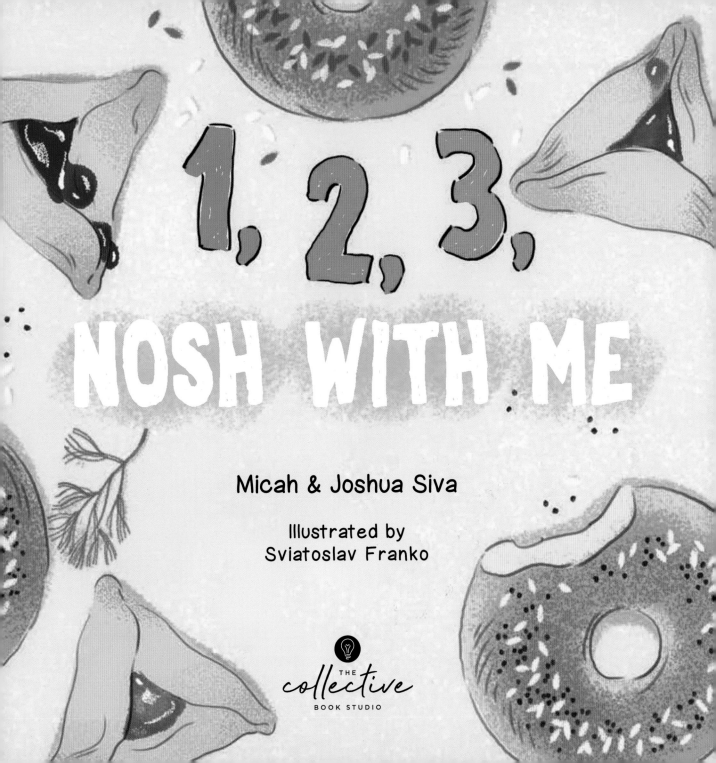

1, 2, 3,
NOSH WITH ME

Micah & Joshua Siva

Illustrated by
Sviatoslav Franko

THE
collective
BOOK STUDIO

Library of Congress Cataloging-in-Publication Data available.

ISBN: 978-1-68555-772-0
Ebook ISBN: 978-1-68555-134-6
LCCN: 2023900235

Printed using Forest Stewardship Council certified stock
from sustainably managed forests.

Written and designed in the USA.
Illustrated in Ukraine.
Manufactured in China.

Design by Andrea Kelly.
Illustrations by Sviatoslav Franko.

1 3 5 7 9 10 8 6 4 2

The Collective Book Studio®
Oakland, California
www.thecollectivebook.studio

To our family, who showed us love through our tummies

My family likes to eat yummy
food together.

Let's count them
one by one!

One golden **challah,**
to celebrate **Shabbat . . .**

(yummy in my tummy!)

1

Two fluffy **matzo balls,**

floating in my **soup**

Three crunchy **matzos,**
on the **seder table**

Four cheesy **kugels**,
packed with oodles of **noodles**

Five flaky **knishes**,
filled with mashed **potatoes**

(mmm mmm good!)

Six crispy **apples,**

dipped in honey for a

Sweet New Year

This ancient painting from a private tomb shows a hippopotamus roaring among papyrus.

be found in Egypt anymore, they once roamed the Nile freely. People went out in boats to hunt them, and the animals could easily capsize boats and injure the people who fell out.

In 2010, Dr. Benson Harer offered up a new theory about King Tut's death. Tutankhamun's body was found with severed ribs and his heart was not embalmed, which was unusual. Dr. Harer believes it is evidence of a crushing injury to the chest. In Tutankhamun's tomb, there are two statues of the young king hunting hippopotamus using a spear. Might this have been King Tut's last act? A run-in with a hippo is a gruesome way to go.

7

Seven sweet **sufganiyot,** stuffed with **tasty jelly**

Eight chewy **bagels,** topped with lots of **schmear**

8

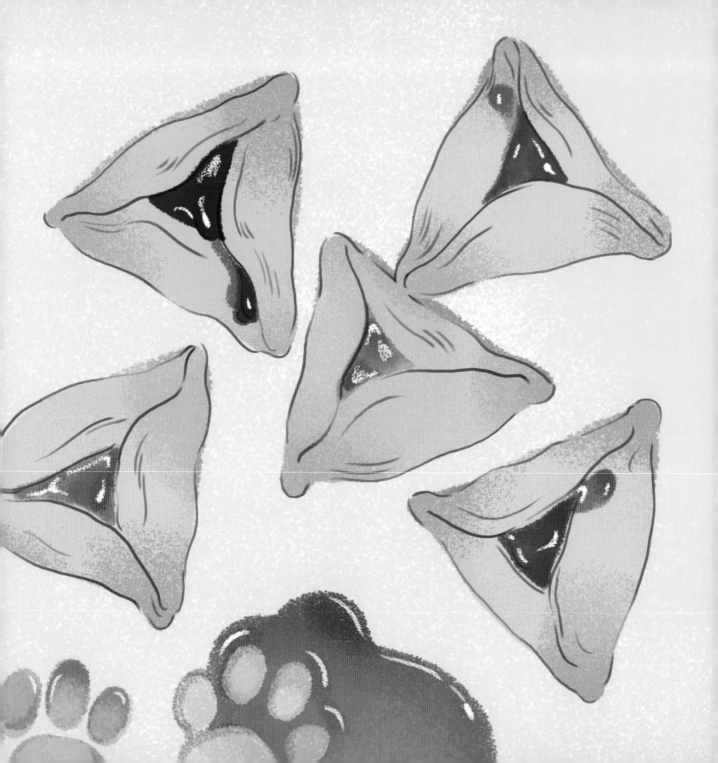

9

Nine **hamantaschen,**
which look like fun pointy **hats,** and

Ten crispy **latkes**,
served by **candlelight!**

10

Foods that are yummy in our **tummy**,

foods that mean **love**,

foods that mean **family**,

and foods to **celebrate**

what makes me, **me!**

Simple Challah

Makes 1 (1½ lb) loaf; 10 to 12 servings

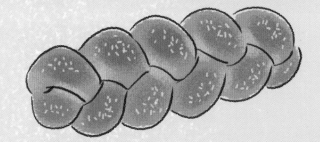

For the dough

3 ¾ cups bread flour, plus more for shaping

2 ¼ teaspoons (1 package) instant yeast

1 teaspoon kosher salt

⅔ cup warm water

3 tablespoons sugar

2 large eggs, at room temperature

3 tablespoons vegetable oil, plus 1 tablespoon for greasing

For the egg wash

1 large egg, whisked

1 tablespoon water

Toppings, optional (see following pages)

To make the dough

1. Oil a large bowl and set it aside.

2. In a large bowl, mix together the flour, yeast, and salt until combined.

3. In a medium bowl, whisk together the water, sugar, eggs, and oil.

4. Pour the wet ingredients into the dry ingredients and mix until a rough dough forms.

5. Lightly flour a work surface. Tip the dough onto the floured work surface and knead until a smooth-soft dough forms, 8 to 10 minutes. (You can also do this in a stand mixer, using the dough hook. Mix on low until smooth, 5 to 10 minutes.)

6. Transfer the dough to the oiled bowl, cover with a damp, clean kitchen towel, and let rise in a warm place until doubled in size, about 1 hour.

7. Preheat the oven to 350°F. Line a baking tray with parchment paper.

8. Lightly flour a work surface. Punch down the dough in the bowl to remove any air bubbles and transfer it to the floured work surface.

To make a braid:

9. Cut the dough into 3 equal pieces (A and B). Roll each piece into a rope (C), about 12 inches long. Cover with a damp cloth and let rest for 10 to 15 minutes.

10. Braid the 3 pieces together, using the illustrations below as a reference and pinching the dough at the ends to seal (D through H). Hide the ends of the dough by tucking them under the braid. Place the braided dough on the parchment-lined baking tray.

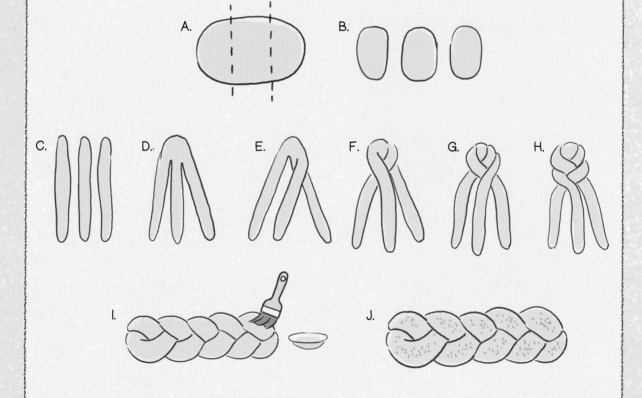

To make the egg wash

11. In a small bowl, whisk together the egg and water. Brush the dough with the egg wash
(see I, previous page).
Sprinkle your favorite toppings over the top, if using (see J, previous page).

To finish

12. Bake for 20 minutes. Turn the tray and bake for another 20 minutes, or until golden brown.
If using a thermometer, it should read 190°F.

To make a coil

Roll the dough into a 30-inch rope, and, using the illustrations as a reference, create a spiral.
Hide the end by tucking it underneath the coil and place it on the baking tray.

A.

B.

C.

D.

E.

F.

G.

COILED

Top the challah with your favorite nuts, seeds, or even sprinkles!

Everything Bagel:
Top with 3 tablespoons of an everything bagel seasoning blend.

Pizza Challah:
Brush with 3 tablespoons tomato sauce instead of the egg wash.
Top with 1/4 cup shredded mozzarella cheese.

Cinnamon Toast:
Mix 2 tablespoons white sugar and 1 teaspoon cinnamon and sprinkle over the top.

Coconut Almond:
Mix 1 tablespoon shredded unsweetened coconut,
2 tablespoons sliced almonds, and 1 teaspoon sugar.
Sprinkle the mixture over the top.

Unicorn Challah:
Top with 4 tablespoons rainbow sprinkles.